4/76

A
STEPPING-
STONE
BOOK

PICTURE
SIGNS
&
SYMBOLS

By
WINIFRED
&
CECIL LUBELL

¿?

PARENTS'
MAGAZINE PRESS
NEW YORK

Library of Congress Cataloging in Publication Data
Lubell, Cecil.
　　　Picture signs and symbols.
　　　(A Stepping-stone book)
　　　SUMMARY: Explains the use of picture signs and
symbols as a form of communication.
　　　1. Signs and symbols—Juvenile literature.
[1.Signs and symbols]　　I. Lubell, Winifred, joint
author.　　II. Title.
AZ108.L82　　　001.55'2　　　76-39742
ISBN 0-8193-0577-4 (lib. bdg.)

Contents

1. Look At All the Signs 4

2. This Way to the Elephants 10

3. One Language for Everyone 14

4. Signs Are Shortcuts 16

5. Signs for Drivers 18

6. In the Airport 24

7. At the Olympic Games 26

8. Indian Sign Language 28

9. This Hand Is Mine 31

10. A Sign for Peace 33

11. Flags Are Symbols, Too .36

12. Animal Symbols 41

13. Signs of the Cross 45

14. Holiday Symbols 48

15. Shopkeeper Signs 52

16. Follow the Map 54

17. New Symbols 60

18. Are Signs Enough? 62

   Index 63

1. Look At All the Signs

Take a ride into town and this is what
you will see:

Signs. Signs. Everywhere.
All kinds of signs.

All those signs have words, but there's another kind of sign without words. It's a picture sign. It tells you something without spelling it out in letters.

A clock face is a picture sign. It tells you the time.

A traffic signal is also a sign without words. Green says "GO"; yellow says "WAIT"; Red means "STOP."

Here's a different kind of picture sign:

It's the sign on a mailbox. We call it a
symbol, which means that it stands for
something else. The eagle is a symbol of the
United States and the eagle sign tells you
where to find a U.S. mailbox.

Once you start looking around, you begin
to see many signs without words.

Everyone knows what arrow signs mean.
You see them everywhere, in all kinds of shapes
and sizes. And everywhere in the world they
mean the same thing.

Even people who can't read can understand
an arrow. It's a useful sign. It gives you
quick, simple directions such as "TURN RIGHT,"
"GO AROUND THE BEND," "TURN LEFT."

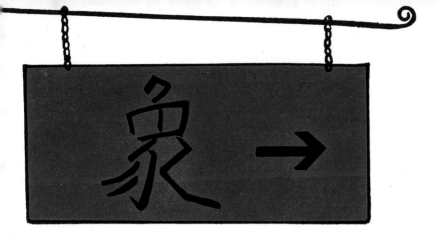

2. This Way to the Elephants

Now let's see how we can use the arrow sign, together with another picture, to show people how to find something without saying it in words.

Let's pretend we are visiting a zoo in a foreign country.

At a zoo in Japan we might see the sign shown at the top of this page.

We can't read Japanese so we don't understand the sign. But here's a sign that says the same thing without words:

Everyone can understand that sign.
In Israel we might see a sign like this:

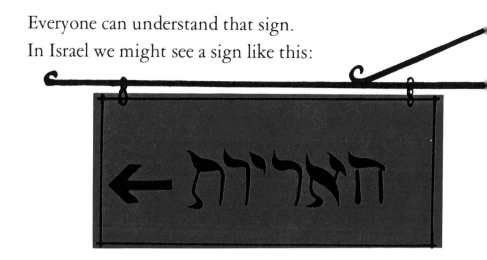

But if we don't understand Hebrew the sign
won't help us. So let's translate it into a
picture sign, like this:

It clearly says: "This way to the lions."

In a Greek zoo we might see this sign:

It says: "To the Monkeys." But it doesn't
mean a thing to someone who can't read Greek.
Here's the same sign in pictures:

In any language these signs say:
"This way to the Birds"..."To the Crocodiles"
..."To the Bears."
And when you're ready to leave the zoo,
here's a picture sign that tells you where to
get the bus.

3. One Language for Everyone

That's the idea behind a sign without words. It's a way of giving information to people who come from foreign countries, and who don't read or speak your language.

We already have many signs and symbols that mean the same things in different parts of the world. For example, musical notes mean the same thing everywhere.

1 2 3 4 5 6 7 8 9 10

On this page are some other signs you will probably know.

!	Exclamation point	**+**	Plus
?	Question mark	**—**	Minus
,	Comma	**=**	Equals
:	Colon	**;**	Semicolon
÷	Divided by	**.**	Period
✕	Multiplied by	**&**	And
( )	Parentheses	**$**	Dollars
%	Percent	**#**	Number

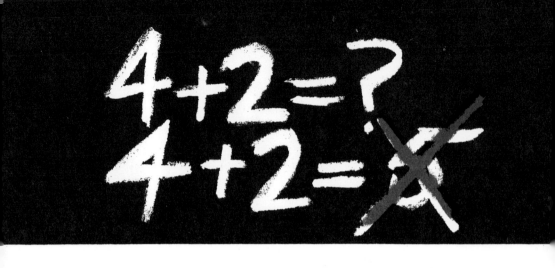

4. Signs Are Shortcuts

Perhaps you didn't think of the marks on
page 15 as signs. But they really are signs.
They give us directions or information
without using letters and words.

They are different from letters, which are
also signs. Letters stand for the sounds
we put together to make words when we speak
to each other. For example, a question mark
(?) doesn't stand for a sound, as do the
letter signs A B C. The question mark tells
us that the words in front of this mark should
be read as a question.

$$7 + 2 = ?$$
$$7 + 2 = 9 \checkmark$$

Of course, we have to agree on these signs and then learn them in order to know what they mean when we see them.

For example, everybody had to agree that the sign $+$ means "plus" and that the sign $=$ means "equals." People also had to learn the numbers 1 through 10. Then, if we write

$$6 + 3 = 9$$

everybody knows it means: "Six plus three equals nine."

You can see that signs and symbols are also shortcuts for saying something quickly.

That's the reason they are used a great deal on roads, especially on superhighways.

5. Signs for Drivers

Cars travel fast today.

It's often hard to read a word sign when you're zipping along at 60 or 70 miles an hour. It's especially hard for the driver who has to keep eyes on the road. And suppose you're in a foreign country and don't understand the language. In that case a word sign doesn't help you at all.

You need a clear sign without words.

Below is a sign like that.

It's easy to see, and everyone can understand it—once they are told what it means.

The thick black line stands for something crossed out, the way your teacher sometimes crosses out a word you spelled wrong:

Br̶ite Bright

This black line in a red circle is used in many parts of the world as a traffic sign. It means: "NO!" or "DON'T GO THIS WAY!"

Now see how neatly it can be used in a road sign to tell you something you want to know.

Let's suppose you are in a car that is
moving very fast on a superhighway. You
are hungry. You see a service center up ahead
and you want to know whether or not it has a
restaurant. Before you reach the service
center you see this sign:

It means: "You can get a cup of coffee here
but no food." There is no restaurant at that
service center.

A little farther on there's another sign:

This one means: "There's a restaurant 6 miles ahead. Also telephone and gas."

Here are some other road signs:

 Winding road ahead.

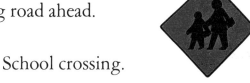 School crossing.

Do not enter.

 Bicycle path.

 Men working ahead.

 Cattle crossing.

In Europe there are many more picture signs on the roads than we have in the United States. Here are some of them:

 You are coming to a main road.

Traffic is joining this road up ahead from the left.

 This road is uneven.

Falling rocks. Watch out!

 The road is going to become narrower.

This road is slippery.

 Watch out for riverbank-dock.

Traffic circle ahead.

No passing.

Steep hill downward.

No left turn.

There are picture signs inside many cars as well. Without using words they make it easy to learn how to operate the car. Here are some you often see on the dashboard:

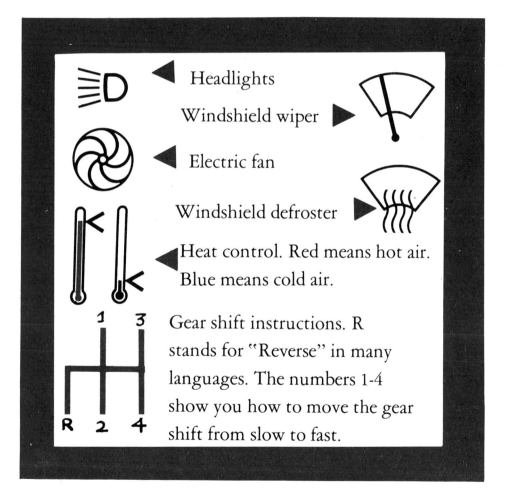

Headlights

Windshield wiper

Electric fan

Windshield defroster

Heat control. Red means hot air. Blue means cold air.

Gear shift instructions. R stands for "Reverse" in many languages. The numbers 1-4 show you how to move the gear shift from slow to fast.

EXIT

NO ENTRY

RESTAURANT

LOCKER

TELEPHONE

SMOKING

NO SMOKING

FIRST AID

6. In the Airport

One place where picture signs are especially helpful to people is at an international airport. Travelers arrive from many parts of the world and often they can't understand the language of the country.

Here are some of the signs you may see at international airports in many countries today:

LOST CHILDREN   MEN'S TOILET   WOMEN'S TOILET

BUS   TAXI   STAIRWAY

BAGGAGE   LOST & FOUND   BANK

Perhaps you can think of some other signs
that would be helpful at an airport.

MAIL   INFORMATION

SYMBOL FOR THE OLYMPICS

7. At the Olympic Games

Another place we need signs without words is at the Olympic Games. They are held in different places each time, and the contestants come from many different lands. Many of them can't understand the language of the country where the Games are being held so picture signs are put up to help them.

Here are some of the signs used at the 1964 Olympic Games in Tokyo, Japan:

GYMNASTICS

SWIMMING

FOOTBALL

BASKETBALL

FENCING

ROWING

WEIGHT LIFTING

BOXING

WRESTLING

BASKETBALL SWIMMING WRESTLING

RIDING FENCING SAILING

Here are different signs invented for the
1968 Olympics in Mexico and the 1972 Winter
Sports Olympics in Sapporo, Japan:

BOBSLEDDING

FIGURE SKATING

SKI JUMPING

CROSS-COUNTRY SKIING

ICE HOCKEY

8. Indian Sign Language

American Indians used signs like those at the Olympics long before white men came here. They knew how to tell a whole story in picture signs without words.

Here is a sentence in English, followed by the picture signs an Indian might have used to write the same sentence:

"At sunrise three men left the camp beside the lake to hunt deer, because they were hungry."

At sunrise *(sun in the east)*
three men
left camp *(footsteps going away from wigwams)*
beside the lake *(stream going in and out of lake)*
to hunt *(with an arrow)*
deer *(which have antlers)*
because they were hungry. *(line across belly to show it is empty.)*

Here are three picture sign messages left
by an Indian who lived alone in Maine many
years ago. He scratched these messages on
birch bark. Then he rolled it up and tied it to
his wigwam so that his friends would know
where he had gone.

This means: "I am going across the lake to
hunt deer."

This says: "I am going toward the lake,
but will turn where there is a pointer before
reaching the lake."

The third message means: "I am going
hunting and will be gone all winter." This is
shown by the sled and the snowshoes.

The Indians of Alaska also used picture signs
to tell a story. They carved tiny figures on
pieces of ivory or wood.

Here is a drawing of a picture carving in
which an Indian tells the story of a hunt. It
shows him leaving his house and then tells how
many animals he caught. All the animals he
caught have their heads pointing to his house.
The ones he did not catch are facing away
from the house. He caught one wolf, two deer,
and three beavers. The ones that got away
were a porcupine, a seal, and a fox.

9. This Hand Is Mine

Long, long ago, before man invented letters and an alphabet, people also used signs like those made by the Indians.

Here is a sign found on the wall of an ancient ruined house in Turkey.

This sign of a hand was put there by a house builder almost ten thousand years ago. Why?

Perhaps he thought it would protect his house from robbers. Even today we use the sign of a hand to say "Stop!" or "Stay Out!"

A first-aid sign.　　　A V-for Victory sign.　　　A stop sign.

Or perhaps he painted a picture of his own hand for the same reason we paint our names on a house sign. He may have been saying: "Here is a picture of my hand to show that this house is mine."

Remember, he didn't know how to write, but he did know how to make a print of his hand. Since no man's hand is exactly like any other, this was truly his very own sign.

On this page are some of the hand signs we use today:

A sign for brotherhood.　　　A printer's sign, used instead of an arrow.

10. A Sign for Peace

Of course, we can't be sure what the hand
sign meant so many thousand years ago. We can
only guess, since we can't talk to the man
who made it.

The only way we can be sure about the meaning
of any picture sign is when everybody agrees
on its meaning. That's why picture signs must
be easy to understand.

We must also get used to seeing them so
that we can recognize them immediately.

Here's an example of a sign many people are
now getting used to seeing:

And here's another:

Both these signs stand for peace all over the world today. The second one is a fairly new sign, only a few years old, and this is the way it came about.

The new peace symbol comes from the language of flag signals which were used by ships at sea, before the days of radio, to send messages to each other. A sailor stood on deck with a flag in each hand. He would move the flags into different positions and each position spelled out a different letter of the alphabet. In that way he could spell out words and sentences which would be understood by sailors on another ship.

For example, this is the way flag signals would spell out the word FIRE:

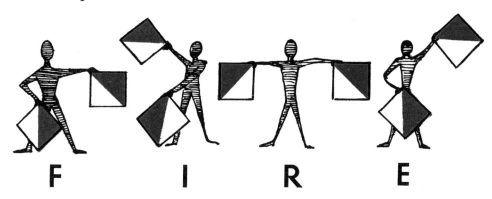

F   **I**   **R**   **E**

Now look at the peace sign again. It's made up of two flag signal letters—N and D.

This is **N**:   or

This is **D**:   or

Together they make **ND**:   or ⅄

ND stands for *Nuclear Disarmament.*

The circle means "The Whole" or "Total." ◯

So this sign without words means: ☮

"TOTAL NUCLEAR DISARMAMENT."

And that stands for PEACE. You can't have war without weapons.

11. Flags Are Symbols, Too

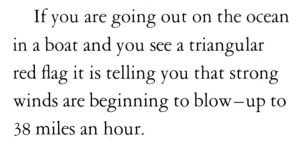

If you are going out on the ocean in a boat and you see a triangular red flag it is telling you that strong winds are beginning to blow—up to 38 miles an hour.

If you see two triangular red flags on the same stick it means the winds are even stronger—up to 54 miles an hour—and you'd better stay on shore.

When you see a square red flag flying from a boat, it means the boat is in trouble and needs help. A similar red flag at the end of a truck means "DANGER. STAY AWAY." And on a skating rink it means "DANGER. THIN ICE."

In ancient times a red flag was the flag of pirates and was a symbol of rebellion.

And, of course, this flag is also a sign. It's the sign of the United States. The 50 white stars on blue stand for the 50 states, and the 13 red and white stripes stand for the 13 original colonies.

Each independent country in the world now has a flag of its own. It wasn't always that way. Flags did not begin to be popular until about 1,400 years ago.

Sad to say, these colorful emblems were almost always signs of war. In ancient times soldiers wore armor in battle and they all looked very much alike. In order to recognize one side from the other each side carried a different flag. Often each knight had his own special flag which helped to identify him and his men during battle.

When modern nations began to develop about 600 years ago the many separate flags disappeared. Instead, each country chose one flag for all its people. Today there are more than 150 national flags in the world.

Here are a few national flags to show you how some of these symbols came about. There is a story and a reason behind each one of these, as there is behind the U.S. flag.

CANADA

When Canada became independent of England in 1964, the Canadian government chose this flag because the maple leaf is the national symbol of Canada. Before they decided on it they looked at 4,000 other designs.

38

LAOS

Laos was once known as the land of a million elephants, and that explains the sign of the elephant on its flag. It has three heads which stand for the three parts of the kingdom in ancient times, now united into one. Over the elephant is the sign of a white umbrella which stands for royalty. The five lines underneath represent the first five commandments of Buddhism, which is the religion of the country.

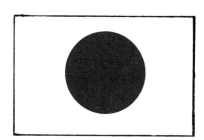

JAPAN

The white flag of Japan has a red circle that stands for the sun. It is the ancient Japanese symbol for the Sun Goddess who is said to have created the island of Japan.

U.S.S.R.

The sign of Russia, the U.S.S.R., is a red
and gold flag. It was adopted in 1923 when
the Soviet government came to power after a
revolution. The red ground stands for
revolution. The gold hammer and sickle stand
for a union of workers and farmers.

TURKEY

The red Turkish flag shows a yellow star
and crescent, which are ancient Moslem symbols.
This is the main religion of Turkey.

UNITED NATIONS

The United Nations flag is blue and white.
It shows a map of the world and two olive
branches, an ancient peace symbol. Peace
among the nations of the world is the hope of
all people everywhere.

12. Animal Symbols

A bear can be a sign and a symbol. So can a bird, a snake, a fish, or any one of a hundred different creatures. Animals have been used as symbols since very ancient times and they are still used in the same way today.

A donkey is the symbol of the Democrats. An elephant is the symbol of the Republicans. An eagle is used on the seal of the U.S.

The sign of Smokey the Bear is used as a warning against forest fires in our parks.

Think of all the sports teams that use animals
for their names and signs. In baseball there
are the Baltimore *Orioles*, the Chicago *Cubs*,
the Detroit *Tigers*, and the St. Louis *Cardinals*.
In football we have the Atlanta *Falcons*, the
Baltimore *Colts*, the Los Angeles *Rams*, and the
Miami *Dolphins*. In basketball there are the
Atlanta *Hawks*, the Chicago *Bulls*, and the
Milwaukee *Bucks*. In hockey, the Boston *Bruins*.

Among the American Indians, animals were
used as magic signs. Each group or clan had
its own special animal whose picture was carved
or painted on houses and totem poles. The
members of a clan never hunted or killed the
animal they took for their special sign because
they believed it was a powerful protector and
would keep them from harm, or bring good luck.

Some of this feeling about animals has come
down to us today. We say:

"As smart as a fox." "As strong as a bear."
"As quick as a bird." "As slow as a turtle."
"As fast as a hare." "As busy as a bee."
"As wise as an owl." "As gentle as a lamb."
"As peaceful as a dove." "As brave as a lion."

Because we think of these animals in this
way we often use their pictures as symbols in
the same way we use the picture of a dove as
a symbol of peace in the world.

Long ago, imaginary animals were also used
as symbols. The dragon was one of these. No
such creature ever existed. It was invented as a
symbol of evil, except in China where it was once a
symbol of the Emperor's power. Today it's a Chinese
sign for the new year.

Another imaginary creature was the griffin,
half eagle and half lion. It was the symbol of
a good spirit, a guardian protector of life.

And then there was the thunderbird, an
imaginary bird invented by the Indians. They
believed it caused thunder and lightning. Today
it's become the symbol of one automobile.

13. Signs of the Cross

Sometimes a sign has more than one meaning.

Look at this one:

It can mean "X marks the spot"

or "Love and Kisses"

or "A mistake"

or "Multiplied by"

or "A railroad crossing."

Turn it a little and it becomes a different kind of cross altogether:

In this shape it can mean "Plus"

or "First Aid"

or "Cross Road."

For the American Indians a cross like this
was a sign of good luck, or hope, or wisdom.
It is a very ancient symbol, used thousands of
years ago by the people of the Far East. And
it always stood for something good.

But then the Nazis in Germany made it into
an evil sign. They turned it sideways, like this,

and it became the symbol of a government
that murdered millions of people and brought
on a terrible world war.

Here is a different cross:

It stands for the Christian religion because
Jesus Christ was crucified on a wooden cross
of that shape.

Other religions have different symbols.
This six-pointed star is the
sign of the Jewish religion. It
is called the Star of David,
because he was King of the Jews
in ancient times.

This symbol stands for the
Moslem religion of the Arab
peoples in the countries of
the Near East.

This wheel is the symbol of
Buddhism, the religion of many
people in the Far East.

Here is the symbol for
Hinduism, the chief religion
of India.

And this is the symbol for the
Shinto religion in Japan.

14. Holiday Symbols

You don't need words to tell you what these signs mean.

Everybody knows that they mean Christmas— December 25. Even before it was a festival of Christ it was also a winter holiday of lights, celebrated to bring some brightness into the darkest time of the year.

Another festival of lights is the Jewish holiday, Chanukah, whose symbol is the Menorah, a candle holder with nine lights.

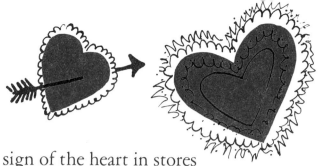

When you see the sign of the heart in stores all over town you know immediately that Valentine's Day is coming on February 14. This was also an ancient holiday held to celebrate the first signs of spring.

And the pumpkin face with a candle inside, or the witch flying on a broomstick, mean one thing to everyone in the U.S.—Halloween.

Each of these holiday symbols—and many more—has a story behind it. Often it's a very ancient story.

The candle-lit pumpkin of Halloween is a symbol of an ancient harvest festival when people used to light bonfires to keep away the ghosts and witches they believed were all around on the night of October 31.

And the colorfully decorated eggs that are
a sign of Easter for us are also symbols of
the springtime festivals that were celebrated
hundreds of years ago. They were meant to be
signs of the new life beginning in nature.

Each country has its own holiday symbols.
In the U.S. we have a Liberty Bell for July 4,
a turkey for Thanksgiving Day, a cherry branch
and hatchet for Washington's Birthday, and a
log cabin for Lincoln's Birthday.

In Japan there are two spring festivals.
The Festival of the Kites (May 5) is for boys.
They fly kites in the shapes of fish—a
symbol of strength and bravery. Another is

the Festival of the Dolls when little girls
parade with their new dolls. The symbol of
this festival is a peach blossom.

In China the sign of the new year is a
huge paper dragon which is carried in parades
with thousands of colored lanterns.

And in Sweden the winter festival is St. Lucia's
Day when young girls in white dresses and red
sashes wear crowns of lighted candles and sing
for grownups at parties all over the land.

Signs like these are used in festivals all
over the world. They tell us a lot about the
customs of these lands.

51

СЛÉСАРЬ

15. Shopkeeper Signs

Look at all these shop signs!

Long ago most shopkeepers had picture signs outside their shops. Usually the signs had words painted on them too, but even if people couldn't read the words they could tell just what was sold in each shop.

These store signs are all from different countries, all in different languages. You may not be able to understand the words, but you will certainly know that kind of shop it is from the picture signs.

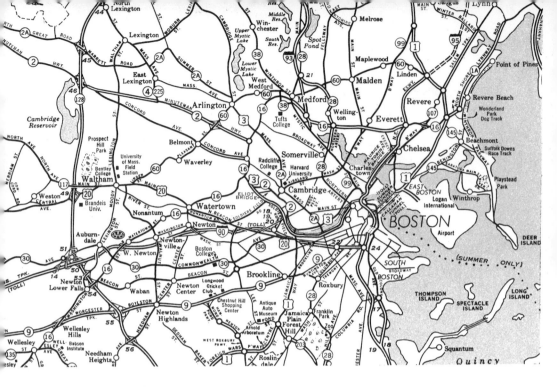

16. Follow the Map

An automobile road map is full of symbols.
Some of them are so small you need a magnifying
glass to see them. It's like a picture puzzle,
but if you look long and carefully you begin
to see a great many signs hidden among the
lines and words and dots and colors.

The first place to look for map signs is in
the space along the sides or bottom of the map.
On some maps this space is marked:

"HOW TO READ THIS MAP."

Here are some of the signs you will see:

This sign tells you the direction
for North, South, East, and West.
It's usually a big sign placed
in an empty part of the map.

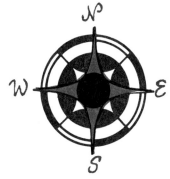

An unpaved dirt road.

Both these signs mean good
roads. The red one stands
for a superhighway.

U.S. highway.

State highway.

Interstate highway.

Ski area.

Fish hatchery.

┼┼┼┼┼┼┼┼┼┼┼┼	A railroad line.
⩓	Bridge over river or stream.
⟶✗▭✗⟶	A drawbridge.
⟶⊢┄┤⊢⟶	A tunnel.
✈	An airport.
🏕	A campsite.
🌲🌲🌲	State park.
🌊	Blue area for a lake.
∿	Blue line for river or stream.
⛪	A church.
•—5—•	Shows the distance in miles between two points on a road.

A swamp.	
A sand area.	
Water.	
Electric line, with towers.	

And here are six different signs which show how many people there are in a town:

Less than 500 people.	O
500 to 2,500.	⊙
2,500 to 5,000.	⓪
5,000 to 10,000.	◉
This means a state capital.	★
A yellow area means a city of more than 10,000 people.	

Little Bay

Here's a map which shows how some of these symbols are used to give you information.
See if you can figure them all out.

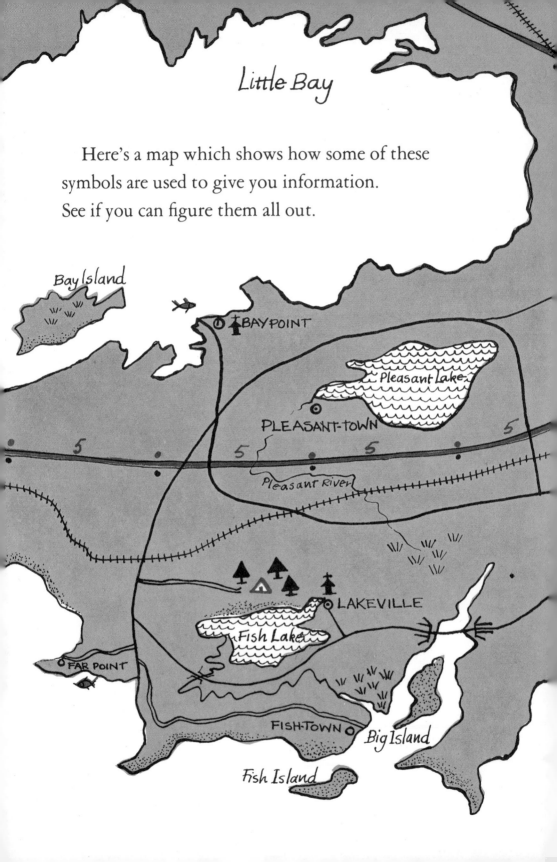

Bay Island

BAY POINT

Pleasant Lake

PLEASANT-TOWN

5　　　5　　　5　　　5

Pleasant River

LAKEVILLE

Fish Lake

FAR POINT

FISH-TOWN

Big Island

Fish Island

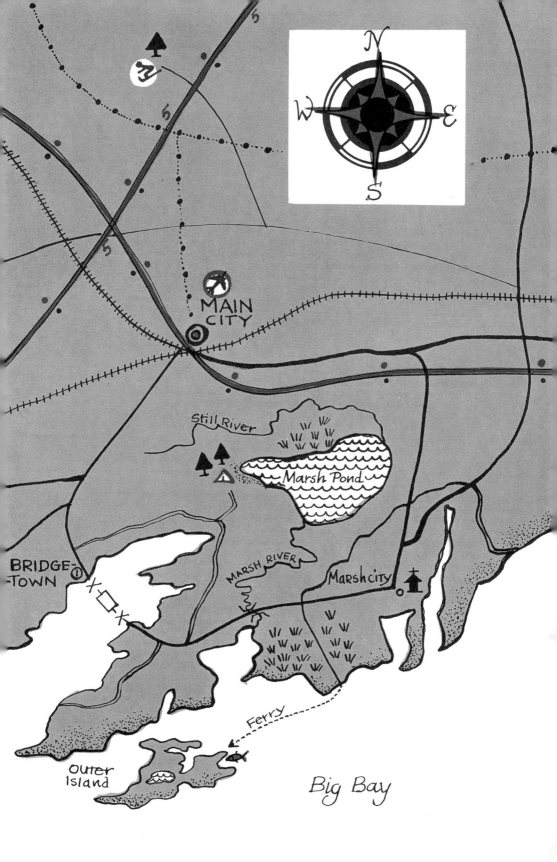

17. New Symbols

New picture signs and symbols are created
all the time. If you join a club it almost
always has a special symbol which you can wear
as a pin, like the sign for the Boy Scouts or
the Girl Scouts. And if you start a club of
your own you will probably want a sign of your
own and you may very well pick an animal sign,
as the Indians did long ago.

The supermarket shelves are full of signs
on packages, put there by the manufacturers so
that you will recognize the package quickly.

There are new signs and symbols for inventions
and discoveries, like the symbol for atomic
energy which is now used by scientists all
over the world.

And here are some signs you may never have seen before. They will soon be used in many countries by people who hope to save the world from pollution. They are the new signs for ECOLOGY, which means the protection of this planet earth from pollution of every kind.

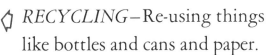

This is the sign for *ECOLOGY.*

RECYCLING—Re-using things like bottles and cans and paper.

NOISE—Making the world a quieter place to live in.

AIR—Keeping the air fit to breathe.

POPULATION—Not having too many people on the earth.

WATER—Clean water, free from pollution.

LAND—Healthy land, good for growing things.

18. Are Signs Enough?

Signs without words can tell us a lot—as you have seen in the pages of this book. But picture signs cannot take the place of words altogether. With words we can express ideas and thoughts. We can't do that very well just with picture signs.

For example, thousands of years ago people lived in caves and left picture signs on the cave walls. But these people did not know how to write, so they could put down very little about their lives and nothing at all about their thoughts. We can only guess at this.

It's the same today. If we want to find out about history, or write poetry, or tell other people what we are thinking and feeling, then we need words and language. And not only our own language but also the languages of other countries.

No, signs alone will not give us an international language, but they can point the way.

 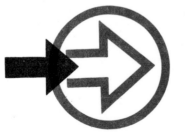  

Index

air, 61
airports, signs in, 24-25
and, 15
animals, signs for, 10-13, 28-30;
    as symbols, 41-44;
    sayings about, 43
arrow signs, 8-13
atomic energy, symbol for, 60
automobiles, see cars

Baggage, 25
Bank, 25
baseball, and animal symbols, 42
basketball, and animal symbols, 42
bears, 13
birds, 13
boats, flag symbols for, 36
Buddhism, 39, 47
bus, sign for, 13, 25

Canada, flag of, 38
cars, signs on dashboards of, 23
Chanukah, symbol of, 48
China, dragon and, 44, 51
Christians, symbol of, 46
Christmas, symbols of, 48
clock face, 6
clubs, signs for, 60
colon, 15
comma, 15
crocodiles, 13
cross, as symbol, 45-46

Democrats, symbol of, 41
division, 15
dollars, 15
"Don't go this way!", 19
dragon, as symbol, 44, 51

eagle, 7, 41
Easter, symbols of, 50
ecology, sign for, 61
equals, 15, 16
exclamation point, 15
Exit, 24

Far East, and cross, 46;
    religion in, 47
Festival of the Dolls, 51
Festival of the Kites, 50
festivals, see holidays
Fire, 35
flag signals, 34-35
flags, as symbols, 36-40
First Aid, 24
football, and animal symbols, 42
Fourth of July, 50

"go," 6
"Go around the bend," 9
green, 6
griffin, as symbol, 44

Halloween, symbols of, 49
Hebrew, sign in, 11
hands, as signs, 31-32
Hinduism, symbol of, 47
hockey, and animal symbols, 42
holidays, symbols for, 48-51

India, religion in, 47
Indians, signs of, 28-30;
    and animal symbols, 43, 44;
    and cross, 46
Information, 25
Israel, zoo sign in, 11

Japan, zoo sign in, 10;
    Olympic Games signs in, 26, 27;
    flag of, 39;
    religion in, 47;
    festivals in, 50-51
Japanese, sign in, 10
Jesus Christ, 46
Jews, symbol of, 47

land, 61
Laos, flag of, 39
Lincoln's birthday, 50
lions, 11
Locker, 24

Lost & Found, 25
Lost Children, 25
Mail, 25
mailbox, sign on, 7
maple leaf, 38
maps, *see* road maps
Men's Toilet, 25
Mexico, Olympic Games signs in, 27
minus, 15
monkeys, 12
Moslems, symbols of, 40, 47
multiplication, 15
musical notes, 14

Nazis, and cross, 46
Near East, religion in, 47
new year, symbol of, 51
No entry, 24
No Smoking, 24
noise, 61
Nuclear Disarmament, 35
number, 15

Olympic Games, signs for, 26-27

parentheses, 15
peace signs, 33-35, 40, 43
percent, 15
period, 15
picture signs, 6, 7, 10-13, 14;
    new, 60-61;
    and words, 62
pirates, and red flag, 36
plus, 15, 16
population, 61
punctuation signs, 15

question mark, 15, 16

recycling, 61
red, 6
religion, 39, 40, 46-47
Republicans, symbol of, 41
restaurant, signs for, 20-21, 24
road maps, signs on, 54-58
road signs, 17-22
Russia, *see* U.S.S.R., 40

St. Lucia's Day, 51
semicolon, 15

Shinto religion, symbol of, 47
shops, signs for, 52-53
shortcuts, signs as, 16-17
signs, definition of, 5-6
signs without words, *see* picture signs
skating rink, red flag and, 36
Smoking, 24
sports teams, symbols of, 42
spring, symbols for, 49, 50-51
Stairway, 25
star, as symbol, 47
Star of David, 47
"Stop," 6
stores, *see* shops
superhighways, *see* road signs
Sweden, winter festival in, 51
symbol, definition of, 7

Taxi, 25
Telephone, 24
Thanksgiving, 50
thunderbird, as symbol, 44
Total Nuclear Disarmament, 35
totem poles, 43
traffic signals, 6
traffic signs, *see* road signs
truck, red flag and, 36
Turkey, flag of, 40
"Turn left," 9
"Turn right," 9

U.S.S.R., flag of, 40
United Nations, flag of, 40
United States, symbol of, 7, 41;
    mailbox, 7;
    flag of, 37

Valentine's Day, symbol of, 49

"wait," 6
war, weapons and, 35;
    flags and, 37
Washington's birthday, 50
water, 61
wheel, as symbol, 47
Women's Toilet, 25

yellow, 6

zoos, signs in, 10-13